The Influencing Style Clock

Stewart Mitchell
Mariana Brkich
Jon Warner

HRD Press, Inc. • Amherst • Massachusetts

Published by: HRD Press, Inc.
                22 Amherst Road
                Amherst, MA 01002
                (800) 822-2801 (U.S. and Canada)
                (413) 253-3488
                (413) 253-3490 (Fax)
                http://www.hrdpress.com

In association with Team Publications.

ISBN: 0-87425-769-7

Cover design by Eileen Klockars
Production services by Anctil Virtual Office

The Influencing Style Clock

PURPOSE

The Influencing Style Clock is a psychometric instrument that has been designed to help you identify the way you influence others at work. The results will provide you with a basis for improving your effectiveness in communicating with and influencing others.

The Influencing Style Clock will help you learn to recognize the four influencing types, develop practical strategies for influencing others in work and non-work situations, and develop a personal action plan for improving your influencing skills.

DIRECTIONS

On the following pages there are 32 statements describing the ways in which people influence others at work. To complete the inventory you will need to carefully read each statement and mark the answer that you consider is most characteristic of your behavior at work (not at home or with friends) on the Answer Sheet.

Choose your answer based on how you see yourself today, not on how you would like yourself to be, or how you once were. There are no right or wrong answers to this inventory. Answer each question candidly; this will produce the most useful information.

For each statement, mark the box in the Answer Sheet that indicates how the statement applies to you. Use the following scale:

SD	**Strongly Disagree** (this is uncharacteristic, I almost never do this)
MD	**Moderately Disagree**
NAD	**Neither Agree or Disagree**
MA	**Moderately Agree**
SA	**Strongly Agree** (this is completely characteristic, I almost always do this)

Example:

	Strongly disagree	Moderately disagree	Neither agree nor disagree	Moderately agree	Strongly agree
"I work out a plan to resolve disagreements"	SD	MD	NAD	~~MA~~	SA

Make sure you answer all the items. Have the Answer Sheet available and turn the page when you are ready to begin.

The Influencing Style Clock

INVENTORY ITEMS

1. I clarify what the other person thinks an appropriate outcome will be.

2. I give assurances that procedures will be followed carefully.

3. I give the other person help and support to make the best decision.

4. I clearly list who should do what, so that an idea can become a reality.

5. I'm honest about explaining the benefits of what we're doing to the other person.

6. I consult with others about their preferred approach.

7. I offer to guide the other person through all the steps in the process.

8. Outside the organization, I promote ideas to people who count.

9. I actively solicit and present the opinions of people from outside the organization.

10. I advise the other person of relevant rules and regulations.

11. I stress that the end results are what we are looking for.

12. I think carefully before I speak, to ensure that I appear knowledgeable.

13. I insist that the project be staffed by people capable of completing it.

14. I stimulate the other person's interest by talking about the future.

15. I praise the other person's approach.

16. I strongly indicate how I expect others to perform.

The Influencing Style Clock

INVENTORY ITEMS

17. I take the time to talk through major difficulties as they are encountered.

18. I caution the other person to conduct a test before going ahead with a major change to procedures.

19. I stimulate the other person's thinking by presenting novel ways to exploit an opportunity.

20. I inform the other person that things are under control.

21. I carefully explain the factors leading to incomplete or incorrect results.

22. I intervene to reach a compromise.

23. I pressure the other person to focus on results.

24. I explain that I value the other person's opinion.

25. I insist that the project details (e.g. goals, timing, people involved) are discussed, beforehand.

26. I energetically promote new ideas to others.

27. I let the other person know that I will exert pressure on them.

28. I counsel the other person to check the details.

29. I easily convince others of the importance and overall benefits of an approach.

30. I push to get the people needed for a project.

31. I concentrate on the "big picture" view of the future.

32. I persuade the other person that I am interested in taking on a challenge.

Interpreting Your Scores

Transfer your scores from the scoring sheet to the Style Clock, below, and then read the analysis on the following pages.

The highest number indicates your **primary influencing style.** If you have two or more numbers that are the same or within three points of each other, consider all of them your primary style. The lowest number identifies your **least used influencing style.**

Your primary influencing style defines the set of behaviors that you most often use to influence others. This does not mean that it is the only influencing style that you use; everyone has the capacity to use any one of the four styles.

SCORE

22

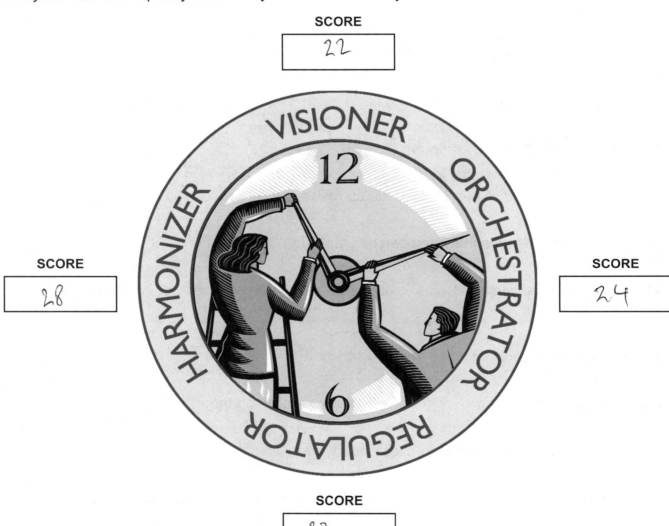

SCORE

28

SCORE

24

SCORE

23

Feedback From Others

If your colleagues (manager, peers, direct reports) were asked to complete the **Influencing Style Clock** about you, record the results here.

Scores of Others	Visioner	Orchestrator	Regulator	Harmonizer
A				
B				
C				
D				
E				
Total Others				
Average Others (divide Total by # of Others)				
Your Score (from page 5)				

Feedback from your colleagues will help you to perceive your impact on others, and highlight what others believe is your **primary influencing style.** Compare **Your Score** with the **Average Others** scores to identify where the scores are most in agreement. Check to see whether your colleagues agree with your assessment of your primary influencing style.

Interpreting the Results

THE VISIONER

Visioners are sometimes viewed as "energy sources" for others. They may appear to be at the center of their own universe. At their best, they are stimulating, creative, able to enthuse others, and create an air of excitement. At their worst, they can overwhelm others with a zealous belief in their own ideas, neither listening to others or considering the full consequences of their actions.

A High Score (30–40) indicates that this is the style you will probably use in your interactions with others. As a strong Visioner, your strengths may be seen as the person who brings ideas and energy to the discussion, while a drawback would be a tendency to be viewed as a social butterfly, flittering from issue to issue without considering anything in real depth. Under stress, the Visioner will exhibit "prima donna" behaviors, and use emotive language, but it will soon blow over.

A Low Score (20–30) indicates that you will use the Visioner approach in conjunction with traits from the other styles. Your strengths will still be viewed as the ability to generate ideas and give alternative viewpoints to routine and often mundane issues, but your creative characteristics will be tempered by either your personal beliefs or a practical nuts-and-bolts approach.

Most of the time you will influence others by your enthusiasm for issues and your ability to visualize several creative solutions to seemingly difficult problems; other times you will influence others by your demonstrated and committed belief in what you are doing, and your ability to promote new ideas.

WAYS YOU CAN IMPROVE AS AN INFLUENCER

Visioners must remember the three key rules: Listen, listen, and listen. Do not let enthusiasm for your own ideas block out the views of others. By slowing down your conversation and giving time to the other person to respond, your ability to influence that person will be enhanced. Remember, the difference between being viewed as enthusiastic and overpowering is the fine line the Visioner walks.

THINGS THAT WOULD DECREASE YOUR INFLUENCING EFFECTIVENESS

Manage your time well: Visioners are not noted for their ability to be on time for meetings and appointments. Don't rush into conversations without getting a feel for the other person's style. Try not to use over-emotive language, such as "I have the most brilliant idea which will just knock your socks off!" As with any style, you will have to control the level of volume for the person you are trying to influence.

Interpreting the Results

THE ORCHESTRATOR

It is hard *not* to notice Orchestrators; action-oriented and independent, they like to get on with things and make things happen. They may be impatient with those that get in their way or slow things down. At their best, they are people who make things happen and get results. At their worst, they appear demanding and inconsiderate toward the feelings of others, even bossy.

A High Score (30–40) indicates that this is the style you will probably use in your interactions with others. As a strong Orchestrator, your strengths may be viewed as the ability to get things done while others play around with details. Some people will be attracted by your decisiveness. However, if used excessively, your style may come across to others as pushy and domineering.

A Low Score (20–30) indicates that you will use the Orchestrator style in conjunction with traits from the other styles. At times, you may be reflective, particularly when considering new ideas, but when you have decided you will move into action mode; other times you may pull back from your action-orientation and focus on the details of the project you are involved with.

WAYS YOU CAN IMPROVE AS AN INFLUENCER

As with other outgoing styles, Orchestrators need to listen actively to others. An often-heard criticism of Orchestrators is that they hear what you say but don't listen to a word. Strong Orchestrators may give the impression that they talk at people, not to them. You can balance this by asking others for their comments or putting your ideas forward as suggestions for discussion, not as a "fait accompli."

THINGS THAT WOULD DECREASE YOUR INFLUENCING EFFECTIVENESS

Orchestrators can decrease their effectiveness by not listening to, ignoring, or giving lip service to the input of others. When others are talking, give them as much positive eye contact as possible and don't look at your watch. Try not to interrupt and don't finish off other people's sentences for them. Before you declare your expectations and charge into action, make sure you have slowed down a little to reflect upon whether you have gathered enough information. This just might help you avoid a few brick walls that didn't need to be knocked down!

Interpreting the Results

THE REGULATOR

Regulators quietly get things done, with an eye for detail and a minimum of fuss. At their best, they are the quiet achievers who can be depended on to deliver the goods, evaluate issues carefully, and get it right. At their worst, they could be seen as being critical of others, pedantic, and resistant to change.

A High Score (30–40) indicates that this is the style you will probably use in your interactions with others. As a strong Regulator, you will be seen as a person who can be relied on to meet deadlines, and who will not overlook the details. Many will value your ability not to be distracted easily from the task at hand, and to focus on what is most important. At times, those strengths will be viewed by some as being too fussy or pedantic, particularly when people are pressuring you for action. Your high standards and need for perfection may frustrate others, as will your lack of enthusiasm for change which is not supported by measurable benefits and detailed plans.

A Low Score (20–30) indicates that you will use the Regulator approach in conjunction with other styles. At times, you may become extremely focused on getting a task right and making sure all the details are considered properly before moving on; others may see this as stubborn and even truculent behavior.

WAYS TO IMPROVE YOUR INFLUENCING

When interacting with people who are enthusiastic about ideas or future opportunities, resist the temptation to ask for detailed information about the plans; share their enthusiasm instead. When dealing with people who are anxious to get on with things, try not to appear as a cynic with 1001 questions, or as lacking in confidence because you tend to be so careful. Match your need for detail with their need for action.

THINGS THAT COULD DECREASE YOUR INFLUENCING EFFECTIVENESS

You may have a strong need for rules and structures (remember, at times there may be issues which transcend these rules); try not to be inflexible in these situations. Your drive for perfection may transfer into your attitude toward others. Keep in mind that your personal standards may not be the same as everyone else's.

Interpreting the Results

THE HARMONIZER

Harmonizers are quiet people, with a strong sense of right and wrong. They are good listeners who enjoy the role of supporting others. As the name suggests, they value harmony in their relationships. At their best, they can be the quiet key stones for relationships; at their worst they can be oversensitive to criticism, resistant to change, and equivocal in their decision making.

A High Score (30–40) indicates that this is the style you will probably use in your interactions with others. As a strong Harmonizer, you will always have time to listen to others (even when you can't spare it). You will empathize easily with others, and will be viewed as someone to be trusted with personal issues. These strengths may be perceived as being too focused on the soft issues. Your need for everyone to be comfortable with decisions may frustrate others, as could a tendency to take issues personally.

A Low Score (20–30) indicates that you will use the Harmonizer approach in conjunction with other styles. At times, you may move into action only after you feel comfortable with an issue or the direction you have taken. In this mode it will be difficult for others to dissuade you from your path once your mind is made up. At other times, you may operate in the world of ideas, engrossing yourself in new information, oblivious to timelines, and even solid reasons for doing what you are doing.

WAYS TO IMPROVE YOUR INFLUENCING

Remember, your strengths lie in the ability to empathize with others; understanding their feelings. Beware of slipping into sympathy (actually feeling what they feel), since this can be self-defeating. Try not to extend yourself, but rather try to get people to help themselves. When you make decisions based on your own values, develop objective criteria to support your decisions. Develop strategies for managing your interactions with others or there will be no time for that other important person—you!

THINGS THAT MAY DECREASE YOUR INFLUENCING EFFECTIVENESS

If you always have time for everyone else, you will not necessarily have the right mental framework for helping someone else. Make sure you are emotionally prepared before you counsel someone else, otherwise it may seem that you are just going through the motions.

When discussing issues which are emotional for you, articulate your feelings rather than hiding them. Keep in mind that just because you believe something is right does not necessarily mean that those who require practical, logical information to support reasoning will believe it's right.

Interpreting the Results

IF YOU HAVE 2 PRIMARY STYLES

If you have two styles that have equally (or within three points) high scores, it is likely that you will use each of them with about the same frequency. This indicates that you are flexible in the way you influence others.

Harmonizer and Orchestrator

You are someone who places importance on traditional values, and are generally conservative in your views. You bring a logical approach to everything you do, and refuse to be rushed into things, particularly when you see it as change for change's sake. At times you may work independently, displaying a "If you want a job done properly, do it yourself" attitude. You also value relationships with others, and on issues of personal beliefs will be resolute in their defense.

Others may see you as independent, perhaps even aloof, but someone who can be relied upon in matters of principle and to stick to agreed upon outcomes.

Regulator and Harmonizer

You are someone who tends to be reserved in the company of others, and who is quite sensitive and sympathetic to other people's needs. You have a high need for orderliness, and feel uncomfortable when your routine is broken. You will often do things to keep the peace rather than to face conflict. At times, you will become engrossed in the detail of what you are doing and may not be aware of issues outside your direct field of focus. You generally like to work with others, but prefer quieter roles where you are not the center of attention.

Others may see you as loyal and dependable; someone who can stick to the task without distraction. Only those close to you will ever get to know "the real you."

Visioner and Orchestrator

You are someone who is results-oriented, and who equally enjoys and needs the excitement of new ideas and the recognition that comes with them. At times, you may be focused on results and display some impatience with those that don't have the same drive. On other occasions, you may be more inclined to quietly listen and be persuaded by others.

Others may see you as a person who is exciting and fun to be with, has considerable drive, and an interest in people's needs and aspirations.

Interpreting the Results

Visioner and Regulator

You are someone who usually enjoys the world of ideas and concepts, and the excitement of fresh challenges. You also enjoy taking a pragmatic approach in turning broad ideas into real results. At times, you may influence others with your persuasive ideas and "big picture" view, but move quickly into the practicalities of getting things done, with the necessary detail.

Others may see you as a person who turns ideas into reality, practically and quickly. Your drive may be viewed as a lack of tolerance for those who may need more time to think things through, and to spend time organizing themselves properly.

Visioner and Harmonizer

You are someone who places a high regard on loyalty and personal values. Your creativity and interest in ideas is matched with a caring approach to and interest in people. At times, you will be the "voice of the people." At the same time, you may avoid argument and confrontation when conflict arrives.

Others may see you as a warm, honest, and creative person who is more concerned with the needs of others than meeting your own personal needs.

Orchestrator and Regulator

You are someone who brings an organized and well-structured approach to almost everything you do. You generally value self discipline in others, and may be less than sympathetic to those who do not exhibit those same traits. At times, your strong focus on producing results, while accepting only the highest of standards, may appear detached, even "cold" in regard to people's feelings.

Others may see you as someone who does not get flustered under pressure. You may also be seen as someone who will deliver results and not take issues personally.

Interpreting the Results

WHEN STYLES ARE IN OPPOSITION TO EACH OTHER

In some instances the two highest-scoring styles may be in opposition to each other. This situation is likely to create a great deal of tension and personal conflict. Orchestrator/Harmonizer and Visioner/Regulator are examples of this.

IF YOUR RESULTS ARE THE SAME FOR ALL FOUR STYLES

If your scores for four styles are within three points of each other, you are able to use the strengths of each style. People who have an even balance over the four styles should find it easier to "style-flex" to an influencing style that is needed or appropriate to the situation.

However, since you have no strong preference for using one type of influencing style, your impact as an influencer may be diffused. Others may find it hard to read and understand you, because you do not demonstrate one dominant style.

If your scores are similar on all four influencing styles you may:

- Have used a "5" rating on most items

- Not seriously considered the effect you have on others when your behavior is inconsistent or unpredictable

- Not answered the items carefully or candidly.

The Influencing Style Clock
Answer Sheet

Using a ball-point pen, firmly mark the box that best represents your answer.

	Rating Scale			
Strongly Disagree	Moderately Disagree	Neither Agree or Disagree	Moderately Agree	Strongly Agree

#					
1.	SD	MD	NAD	(MA)	SA
2.	SD	MD	(NAD)	MA	SA
3.	SD	MD	NAD	(MA)	SA
4.	SD	(MD)	NAD	MA	SA
5.	SD	MD	(NAD)	MA	SA
6.	SD	MD	NAD	(MA)	SA
7.	SD	MD	(NAD)	MA	SA
8.	SD	MD	NAD	(MA)	SA
9.	SD	MD	NAD	(MA)	SA
10.	SD	MD	NAD	(MA)	SA
11.	SD	MD	NAD	(MA)	SA
12.	SD	(MD)	NAD	MA	SA
13.	SD	MD	(NAD)	MA	SA
14.	(SD)	MD	NAD	MA	SA
15.	SD	MD	NAD	MA	(SA)
16.	SD	MD	(NAD)	MA	SA
17.	SD	(MD)	NAD	MA	SA
18.	SD	MD	(NAD)	MA	SA
19.	SD	MD	(NAD)	MA	SA
20.	SD	MD	(NAD)	MA	SA
21.	SD	MD	NAD	(MA)	SA
22.	SD	MD	(NAD)	MA	SA
23.	SD	MD	(NAD)	MA	SA
24.	SD	MD	NAD	MA	(SA)
25.	SD	MD	(NAD)	MA	SA
26.	SD	(MD)	NAD	(MA)	SA
27.	SD	MD	(NAD)	MA	SA
28.	(SD)	MD	NAD	MA	SA
29.	SD	(MD)	NAD	(MA)	SA
30.	SD	(MD)	NAD	(MA)	SA
31.	(SD)	MD	NAD	MA	SA
32.	SD	MD	(NAD)	MA	SA

When completed, separate this form at the edges and follow the instructions for scoring

The Influencing Style Clock
Scoring Sheet

Transfer the numerical scores from this column to the blank boxes in the right-hand column.

#	1	2	3	4	5		Visioner	Orchestrator	Regulator	Harmonizer
1.	1	2	3	④	5					4
2.	1	2	③	4	5				3	
3.	1	2	3	④	5					4
4.	1	②	3	4	5			2		
5.	1	2	③	4	5					3
6.	1	2	3	④	5					4
7.	1	2	③	4	5				3	
8.	1	2	3	④	5		4			
9.	1	2	3	④	5		4			
10.	1	2	3	④	5				4	
11.	1	2	3	④	5			4		
12.	1	②	3	4	5				2	
13.	1	2	③	4	5			2		
14.	①	2	3	4	5		1			
15.	1	2	3	4	⑤					5
16.	1	2	③	4	5			3		
17.	1	②	3	4	5					2
18.	1	2	③	4	5				3	
19.	1	2	③	4	5		3			
20.	1	2	③	4	5				3	
21.	1	2	3	④	5				4	
22.	1	2	③	4	5					3
23.	1	2	③	4	5			3		
24.	1	2	3	4	⑤					5
25.	1	2	③	4	5			3		
26.	1	②	3	④	5		4			
27.	1	2	③	4	5			3		
28.	①	2	3	4	5				1	
29.	1	②	3	④	5		2			
30.	1	②	3	④	5			4		
31.	①	2	3	4	5		1			
32.	1	2	③	4	5		3			
TOTALS: Add scores down. →							**22**	**24**	**23**	**28**

Transfer the scores to the appropriate boxes on page 4 of your *Influencing Style Clock* booklet.

Individual Development Plan

1. My primary influencing style is: _____

2. My strengths show up in the following ways at work (i.e. contribute to effectiveness in my current position):

   _____

   _____

3. My strengths show up in the following ways in non-work situations (i.e. important to achieving my personal goals):

   _____

   _____

4. Building on your influencing strengths:

The skills I want to use more	My action plan (activities on the job, reading, seminars)	Others I will need to involve (manager, peers, direct reports, customers, family, friends)	Completion Date
Skill: Objective:			
Skill: Objective:			

5. Broadening my repertoire of influencing skills:

The skills I want to use more	My action plan (activities on the job, reading, seminars)	Others I will need to involve (manager, peers, direct reports, customers, family, friends)	Completion Date
Skill: Objective:			
Skill: Objective:			

6. The steps I need to take to implement my plan:

   _____

   _____

RESOURCES FOR IMPROVING YOUR INFLUENCING SKILLS

Alberti, R.E., & Emmons, M.L. (1982) **Your perfect right.** San Luis Obispo, CA: Impact Publishers.

Bellman, G.M. (1992) **Getting things done when you are not in charge.** San Francisco: Berrett-Hoehler Publishers, Inc.

Bower, S.A. & Bower, G. (1980) **Asserting yourself: A practical guide for positive change.** Reading, MA: Addison Wesley.

Caroselli, M. (1999) **The Manager's Pocket Guide to Influence with Integrity.** Amherst, MA: HRD Press.

Cohen, A.C., & Bradford, D.L. (1991) **Influence without authority.** New York: John Wiley & Sons.

Decker, B. (1992) **You've got to be believed to be heard.** New York: St. Martin's Press.

Garner, A. (1991) **Conversationally speaking: Tested new ways to increase your personal and social effectiveness.** New York: McGraw Hill.

Kennedy, Gavin (1994) **Field guide to negotiation.** New York: McGraw Hill.

Milo, F. (1990) **How to run a successful meeting in half the time.** New York: Simon & Schuster.

Snyder, Elayne (1990) **Persuasive business speaking.** New York: AMACOM.

Shelton, N. & Burton, S. (1993) **Assertiveness skills.** Boston: Business One—Irwin/Mirror Press.

Zuker, E. (1983) **Mastering assertiveness skills: Power and positive influence at work.** New York: AMACOM.

ABOUT THE AUTHORS

Stewart Mitchell is a management consultant based in Adelaide, South Australia. He has 20 years experience as an adult educator, human resource specialist, and private consultant. Stewart is principal of his own consultancy business specializing in team development and organizational learning. The main focus of Stewart's work is improvement through people. For more than a decade, Stewart has been deeply involved in psychometric assessment programs and training, including accrediting people to apply a variety of psychological assessment instruments.

Mariana Brkich runs a psychological consultancy practice as well as being involved in teaching, research and writing. Her 20 years of professional experience in both the public and private sector has focused on the areas of human resource management and organizational psychology. She has also lectured for a number of years in human resource management and organizational behavior to undergraduate and graduate university students. Mariana's consulting experience has covered areas such as performance management programs, benchmarking, staff attitude surveys, competency frameworks, leadership skills, and career planning and development.

Jon Warner is a senior professional manager with over 20 years experience in a number of major multi-national companies in the United Kingdom, Europe, the United States of America and Australia. This experience has included time as a senior staff manager in human resources and a number of line roles with responsibility for large groups of people. For the last five years Jon has been involved in organizational consultancy and the pursuit of best practice leadership. Jon is also Managing Director of Team Publications Pty Limited, an international training and publishing company committed to bringing practical and fun-to-use learning material to the world-wide training market.